SO YOU MAY
Believe
PART ONE

AN INDUCTIVE BIBLE STUDY
ON THE GOSPEL OF JOHN 1–10

By
Erin H. Warren

contents

start here

The first time I studied John there was a woman named Tammy in my group. She was older and full of so much wisdom. Tammy was facing multiple health challenges, but that just deepened her faith. Each week, I found myself eager to hear the insights she gleaned in that week's study. Though she was a seasoned student of the Bible, she was hungry for more. That hunger fueled my hunger, and I learned so much from Tammy.

Tammy had a knack for understanding the underlying character of God in each passage. The one that impacted me the most was the deliberateness of God. I loved hearing Tammy joyfully exclaim week after week, "He is so deliberate!" More than saying "God's timing is perfect," His deliberate timing in John reminds us of God's purposeful actions. God is specific and clear and orderly. "Deliberate" became one of my top ten favorite characteristics of God. (Okay, who am I kidding? I have way more than ten!)

Tammy was right: the deliberateness of God is evident throughout John. I would even speculate that His deliberate nature rubbed off on John, because John is likewise deliberate in the structure of his Gospel.

Matthew, Mark, and Luke are known as the Synoptic Gospels because they follow a similar narrative order. In fact, scholars believe Mark was written first, and Matthew and Luke expanded his account. John's account of Jesus' earthly life was written last, and it takes a completely different approach. The Synoptic Gospels focus on the events and teachings of Jesus and lean toward reinforcing his humanity (example: Mark often mentions the emotions of Jesus). John focuses on the deity of Jesus, that He is God the Son. Instead of merely telling the events of Jesus' life, John also adds interpretation within the text. He follows a different structure and writes with a deliberate purpose:

> *Now Jesus did many other signs in the presence of the disciples, which are not*
> *written in this book; but these are written so that you may believe that Jesus is*
> *the Christ, the Son of God, and that by believing you may have life in his name.*
> *John 20:30-31*

John clearly and purposefully proves through his Gospel that Jesus is the Son of God, the promised Messiah of the Old Testament, and that He is the only way to eternal life. Each section in John leads to a decision point: will you believe? Or will you walk away? In fact, variations of the word *believe* (i.e., *believed, believes, believing*) occur eighty-five times in John! That's over twice as many occurrences than any other book in the Bible. He uses the background of Jewish institutions and feasts to demonstrate that Jesus is the promised Messiah, which I love because seeing Jesus in the Old Testament is one of my favorite aspects of Bible study.

John also frequently points to Jesus *giving* His life; no one took it from Him. You will see repeated references to Jesus withdrawing when the time was not yet and clear references that show Jesus gave His life for us. Sometimes we tend to think that God sent Jesus to die, and Jesus was reluctant to do so (based on His "take this cup from me" prayer in the Garden of Gethsemane). But Jesus is God. Fully God. God the Son. John reiterates over and over that Jesus and the Father are One, that Jesus is God made flesh (John 1:14), and that Jesus came to do for us what we could not do ourselves.

Oh y'all. I cannot wait to feast on this book with you.

A LITTLE BACKGROUND INFORMATION

Most scholars agree that John's Gospel was written in the AD 90s. A great deal had happened by this point in the first century. The early church experienced intense persecution during the reign of Nero after the Great Fire of Rome, which took place in AD 64. Peter, Paul, and the rest of the disciples had been killed. The Jewish-Roman War took place from AD 66–70, leading to the destruction of the temple in Jerusalem in AD 70. Through it all, Rome remained the major power in the world.

At the time of John's writing, Rome granted the Jewish people a religious amnesty of sorts, meaning that they did not have to bow to the emperor as god and were allowed to practice Judaism and worship in their synagogues. However, the Jewish religious leaders were forcing Jews who converted to Christianity out of the synagogues, meaning they were removed from their protection. As a result, Christians faced persecution not only from the government, but also from their own families and communities. John wanted the original audience to understand that Jesus was more than just another messenger, like Moses or Elijah. He was (and still is) the promised Messiah, the Savior of the world.

THE STRUCTURE OF JOHN

The Gospels are a unique genre because these books are not only narrative, but also theological. The writers tell us stories, but their purpose is to convey truths about Jesus and what we believe about Him. It was common in that day for biographers to arrange these stories out of sequence, which accounts for some of the differences in the four Gospels.

Matthew and Luke begin their accounts with Jesus' birth. Mark starts with the beginning of Jesus' public ministry. But John starts with Genesis.

In the beginning was the Word, and the Word was with God, and the Word was God.
John 1:1

The opening prologue is rich with characteristics of God, and that continues throughout the entire book. John is known for his use of the number seven within the structure of his Gospel, most notably the seven "I AM" statements. These statements capture John's clear intent to demonstrate that Jesus is God as he uses the Greek version of God's personal name, Yahweh (more on that as we study together). John also uses "I AM" seven other times within the book (though not as plainly seen in our English Bibles). There are seven miracles or signs within the book, and a couple other instances of seven we will discover along the way.

The first half of the book (chapters 2-10) uses the backdrop of four icons synonymous with the Jewish faith (a wedding, the temple, a rabbi, and Jacob's well) as well as four major events on the Jewish calendar (Sabbath, Passover, Feast of Tabernacles, and Feast of Dedication) to show how Jesus is the fulfillment of each. This study covers those two sections. The second book covers chapters 11-21, which include the central story in chapters 11-12, the final week of Jesus' life, and the epilogue.

Each week of study, you will write out the repeated words for the week, but for this one, I also want you to note the repeated words across the entire book. Like the theme of belief, there are several key words and phrases that are mentioned over and over. These will help you see the meaning and interpretation and keep the context at the forefront of your mind.

WHY STUDY INDUCTIVELY?

This study is designed to provide a foundation for inductive Bible study. When I first heard of inductive study, I was pretty intimidated. But, it's just a fancy term for studying with your own heart and mind first. I honestly didn't even know I *could* study this way until a few years ago at a conference. I had the privilege of hearing one of my favorite Bible teachers speak, and the following quote from her talk forever changed the way I look at Bible study:

We cannot be content being curators of other people's opinions about a book we can't be bothered to read ourselves. — Jen Wilkin

I realized my entire Christian life I had been a librarian, curating other people's thoughts and beliefs and study findings. It became my driving passion to not only read and study Scripture for myself, but to help other women do the same. I'm so glad you're here! My prayer is that this book helps you:

- Build confidence as you learn how to study the Bible firsthand

- Discover truths about God and His character

- Connect the Old and New Testaments

- Grow in your faith and knowledge in a way that produces life change

- Release the bonds of a "perfect quiet time" to find deeper, richer time in the Word

HOW TO USE THIS STUDY

Feasting on Truth has several levels of studies, and I classify this one as True Inductive. We will use four simple questions (see page 11) to guide our study. Each week will focus on one chapter, and you'll see that the homework includes a guide through those four questions. Under *What Does This Mean?* you'll see some suggested words to look up in the dictionary as well as space to write cross-references (other verses that speak to the same topic or help explain the meaning). There are also a few questions to help kick-start your study but won't cover everything. These are intended to help get you thinking on your own and are not all-inclusive of the meaning. Each week also includes two blank pages for you to make your own notes. I purposely left this section wide open for you, or rather for the Holy Spirit. I want you to have the freedom to take notes in the format you choose: write out specific verses, record observations, make a chart, rewrite commentary quotes or Greek definitions, etc. Each week also includes pages for teaching notes and group notes. I know it can sound intimidating, but I also know you can do it!

Studying a chapter a week is my favorite way to study. I encourage you to read each chapter (and listen to it on your favorite Bible app) over and over throughout the week, then pick a day or two to focus on studying. Always, always start with prayer. Ask the Holy Spirit to guide you in your study time and to reveal truth to you. It's His job (John 14:26; 16:13–15). You'll be amazed at what the Holy Spirit can teach when you give Him the space to speak.

Here are some more tips to help you as you study:

Move Slowly

Many Bible studies plow through Scripture, covering a chapter (or sometimes more) a day. There's certainly a time and a place for that, but I've found when I move through Scripture slowly, reading small sections or focusing on one aspect of the study over the course of one week, the Word of God soaks into my heart and mind deeply. I remember it more easily. I memorize it more effectively. What I love about this particular way of studying is that if I feel the need to stop and let a particular verse sink in, I can do so without feeling like I'm falling behind. It also leaves room for the Holy Spirit to do what only He can do. Which leads me to . . .

Let the Holy Spirit Guide You

Jesus gives us this promise in John 14:26: "But the Helper, the Holy Spirit, whom the Father will send in my name, he will teach you all things and bring to your remembrance all that I have said to you." Anytime I sit down to study, I start with prayer. I ask the Holy Spirit to teach me all the things and to help me remember all the things. That's His job. He's there to help, so invite Him into your time.

Take the Pressure Off

Our time with the Lord doesn't have to be this picture-perfect composition of Bible, notebook, and a cup of coffee (oh how I do love me some good coffee though). The words "quiet time" are not in the Bible, and I've found one size does not fit all. Our time in the Word will change with our stage of life. I tend to deep-dive study about twice a week, but I meditate on it every day. You may sit down and do all of your study in one day or you may devote an hour a day. Find what works for you and stick with it!

Don't Do This Alone

Some of my deepest relationships are ones built on the Word. They are women who gathered around a table or in a living room or online, and we had hard conversations with the Word of Truth between us. Invite a few girlfriends to do this with you. I even included a fun recipe in the back of the book you can make when you get together!

I recommend completing all of the homework on your own before listening to the teaching for the week. You can either listen on your own time or watch together with your group.

Finding time is hard. Women often tell me that they need to put their families first, that work is too crazy, or that they just don't have time to get together with other women for Bible study. Can I challenge you a bit? Is there any time more well spent than investing in our relationship with God? It's hard to pour out from an empty cup. We need to be constantly filled with Jesus, so we can pour out Jesus to our friends, family, and to God. Yes, this may look different in different seasons of life, but you won't regret making it a priority to spend time in the Word with other women.

COMPANION TEACHINGS AND OTHER RESOURCES

I am committed to walking alongside you as you study Scripture inductively. I know you can do this, and I want to help you be successful. Teaching videos are also available to supplement your study. Scan the QR code or visit FeastingOn-Truth.com/John to sign up. You will receive an email with instructions to access the videos. Within the description for each video, you will find links to the podcast version of the teachings as well as *The Alongside Guide*. I have personally curated and put together this valuable study resource for you with cross-references, quotes, characteristics of God, and small group discussion questions. It's everything you need to be successful in your study.

LET'S FEAST

The word *feast* is rooted in abundance, and that's what awaits us in Scripture: a table laid out before us, not only for our essential nourishment, but also for our enjoyment. It is my prayer that the Holy Spirit meets you in the pages of John, and that through this study you will believe and find life in His name.

Happy feasting!

Because of Christ,

Erin H. Warren

four simple questions

Good Bible study is rooted in asking the right questions of Scripture. Our first inclination in Bible study is often to ask, "What does this mean to me?" We want to cut right to the ending. Instead, learning to first understand the context, summary, and character of God in the passage will help us better discern the meaning and our response. I have adopted what I call *Four Simple Questions* as the foundation of my time in the Word. Yes, this takes a little more time and effort, but the practice of persevering through the Word is a valuable one. These four simple questions, as well as other helpful tips and resources for inductive study, are further explained in my book, *Feasting on Truth: Savor the Life-giving Word of God.*

START WITH CONTEXT

It's important to remember that while the Bible was written for us and is applicable to our lives today (Hebrews 4:12), we are not the original audience. It is a book not written in modern America, but in the ancient Middle East. If we do not first answer some key questions to understand the context, we cannot properly understand the passage and its intent. Most of these answers can be found in a good study Bible.

FOUR SIMPLE QUESTIONS

I realized that one of my downfalls when attempting to read and study the Bible for myself was not knowing which questions to ask. Many of the methods I tried were either too open or too rigid. Asking four simple questions provided the right balance of structure and flexibility I needed. I want to release you from thinking this has to look a certain way—it doesn't. Basically: Are you showing up? Are you changing? Are you connected? Does that make you want to keep showing up? If you answer yes to all of these, then you're on the right track! Here is a brief overview of each question:

1. **What does this say?**

   Before we can interpret Scripture, we need to know what's going on in the passage. Some methods would call this *observation* or the *aim of the passage.*

   - Write a 1–2 sentence summary of what the passage is about—no interpretation, just the facts.

   - Answer the questions: Who? What? Where? When?

   - Are there any repeated words or phrases?

   - Are there any transitional words (therefore, so, but, and, etc.)? Remember, every word is there for a reason.

2. **What does this say about God?**

   This to me has been the most transformative question to ask during Bible study. This book is not about us; it's about God. His character and name are written on every page. Before we can understand our response, we must know who He is.

   - What names of God are used? (His names speak to His character.)

   - What characteristics of God are in this passage?

   - I include Jesus in this as well: What does this passage tell us about Jesus?

   - You can find lists of the names and characteristics of God on pages 18–19.

   - Each week, complete the sentence "Because God is _____, I can _____."

3. **What does this mean?**

   PRAY. PRAY. PRAY. Ask the Holy Spirit to guide you in this. Using context, the summary, and other observations you have made, begin to be a detective. Remember the lens through which you are looking. Yes, this takes work, but it's worth doing!

   - Read the passage in multiple translations. What differences do you see?

   - Look up words in the English dictionary.

   - What other passages in Scripture are related to this one? (These are called cross-references.)

   - Read a trusted commentary or study Bible.

   - Research the original language (the Old Testament was originally written in Hebrew and the New Testament in Greek).

   - Go to FeastingOnTruth.com/Resources for recommended resources, Bibles, and commentaries.

4. **How should I respond?**

   Our Bible study should change us. John 17:17 says, "Sanctify them in the truth; your word is truth." *Sanctify* is a big churchy word that means "to purify or to make holy." It's the act of separating ourselves from the actions of our flesh and dedicating more of our lives and actions to God. God's Word has a purpose in our lives (Isaiah 55:10–11), and we shouldn't stop at knowing its meaning. Instead, we should respond:

   - Is there an action I need to take?

- A conversation I need to have?

- A moment of worship?

- Something I should let go?

- Write out a prayer.

However you feel led to respond, write it down and enlist someone to hold you accountable.

OTHER HELPFUL TIPS

Listen to the Passage

Use a Bible app to listen to the passages each week. We often feel like this is a cop-out, but for thousands of years, the Word of God was passed down orally from generation to generation. It's a book meant to be read out loud, and when you listen to it, you'll be amazed at how much you pick up on that you didn't notice when reading it.

Use Different Colored Pens

I've found using different colored pens when writing my study notes helps me remember where the note came from. For instance, I use different colors for rewriting the Scripture verses, my thoughts, certain study Bibles, cross-references or different translations, commentary quotes, and Greek or Hebrew word definitions. I don't really have a color system, so the colors change from time to time. That's okay too!

Start with a Clean Copy of God's Word

A study Bible adds additional commentary. Using a Bible that doesn't have any additional commentary removes the temptation to peek at notes before fully understanding the passage on your own. If you do not have a non-study Bible, don't fret! You can print out chapters on several Bible websites including www.BibleGateway.com. I use an ESV journaling Bible for my initial study (which has very few footnotes), then move to other translations and other study Bibles as I go through my study week. Speaking of translations . . .

A Note About Translations

There are a myriad of translations out there, so how do you know which to pick? First, it's important to know where translations come from. The Old Testament was originally written in Hebrew, while the New Testament was written in Greek (though a few portions of Scripture were written in Aramaic).

Over the years, translators have used original copies written in these languages to interpret Scripture into English (and other languages as well). Translations fall on a spectrum between two ends: word-for-word (translations that use the closest English word to the original word) and thought-for-thought (translations that rephrase the words into more modern, understandable English). Technically, all of them are a mix of the two, but some lean more toward one end or the other.

Some examples of translations that lean toward word-for-word include: English Standard Version (ESV—my top choice), New American Standard Bible (NAS or NASB), and King James Version (KJV). These are the closest to the original language, but we can sometimes miss the cultural context.

An example of thought-for-thought is the New Living Translation (NLT).

There are also versions that are more toward the middle of the spectrum, such as the Christian Standard Bible (CSB) and the New International Version (NIV).

The last kind of translation is not necessarily a translation at all, but rather a paraphrase. Paraphrase Bibles, like *The Message*, should be treated more like commentary because, while they can bring insight into the meaning of the passage, they are not Scripture themselves. I rarely use this type. If you do use a paraphrase, wait until you've completed questions 1–3 and are consulting other commentaries for additional insights.

Welcome to the Feast!

See? Simple. Yes, it takes practice, but honestly, it doesn't take as long as you'd think. You just have to be willing to spend time with Jesus. In Acts 4, Peter and John are on trial before the religious leaders (the smartest of the smart when it came to the Law), and in verse 13 it says, "Now when they saw the boldness of Peter and John, and perceived that they were uneducated, common men, they were astonished. And they recognized that they had been with Jesus." Uneducated. Common. Peter and John hadn't been to seminary, but they had been *with* Jesus.

What I've found is that there is not one method that will make all of this work for you. The power is not in the method. The power is in the Word of God. The power is in spending time with Jesus in the Word with the Holy Spirit as your guide.

When you see your life change and you find community around the Word, you will find yourself returning to Scripture, growing more confident as you study, and discovering the joy and excitement of Feasting on Truth.

Visit FeastingOnTruth.com/HowTo for more information
and in-depth teachings on these questions.

small group guide

I am a firm believer in gathering together around the Word of God. It is at the heart of Feasting on Truth. As stated in *start here*, I believe that small group discussion is incredibly important when studying the Bible. I heard a pastor say, "Our time in the Word should be personal but never private." I do not believe we are called to study in isolation, I believe it is in places of isolation where Satan loves to tempt us. Discussing the passage in a small group setting (even if it's with only one other woman) helps confirm what the Holy Spirit taught us. It holds us accountable to truth. Not only that, but I learn so much from other women too. They will see truths within those passages that I miss. It helps build layers of understanding.

Leading a group is not nearly as difficult as it seems. I like to think of group leaders more like discussion leaders. A great discussion leader talks less than a third of the group time. You may need to speak first or jump in to get the conversation going, but the goal is to get the group talking.

Here are some other tips and a guide for your small group time:

Lead with authenticity
You do not have to have all the answers or have it all together to lead. I do not have it all together, and I fail miserably every day at doing what I know I should (Romans 7!). But I don't have to air all my dirty laundry to be authentic, and I never want my authenticity to enable sin in other people's lives. I've found that when I'm real about where I am and I invite women in to see how God is working on me in those areas, it invites them into authentic life change as well.

Set up a group text or use a group chat app
Connection throughout the week is key to building connection within your group. If you are not tech savvy or keeping up with a group chat isn't your strength, ask someone in the group to take charge of that. It's a great way to get others involved too! Throughout the week, you can check in on your group or share a verse or a particular insight into the passage.

Start with an ice breaker question
It doesn't have to be deep or spiritual, just something to get the conversation flowing. These types of questions are always a great way to help a group of women get to know each other.

Share your summary

Have the women share their summary for that week's passage. Depending on the size of your group, you may want to limit this to two to three women.

Ask: What characteristics of God did you see in this week's passage?

This works well "popcorn style." Let the women jump in with various names and characteristics of God and the verses that correspond. I usually add these to my own notes as well.

Use the weekly discussion questions

There are discussion questions marked within each week's homework. For additional weekly discussion questions, go to FeastingOnTruth.com/John and sign up to receive *The Alongside Guide* in your email. Each week, you'll get additional questions (as well as other resources and notes) delivered right to your inbox.

Share "Because God is" statements

This is a simple one, and I love it when everyone shares theirs! Depending on how long you have been together, some women in your group may not feel comfortable sharing the nitty-gritty of their lives. Having everyone share their "Because God is" statement is a way to engage the women who do not feel comfortable speaking up.

Share prayer requests

Sharing what is going on in our lives opens the door to build community and meet needs. I'll never forget sitting in a group when a woman shared that she needed prayer that she could pass her driving test. Across the table, another woman in the group spoke up and said, "I can help you learn to drive!" A couple months later, I received a picture of the two women holding a brand-new driver's license. It was incredible! Praying for one another is commanded, so allow time for this with your group. Pray with one another. Pray throughout the week. When we do this, we get to share an inheritance in what God is doing through the lives of others.

GROUP LIST

NAME	PHONE	EMAIL

knowing God

For too many years, I struggled with knowing how to interpret Scripture and apply these ancient words to my life. I did not know that God promises to equip us in studying Scripture through the Holy Spirit. And truthfully, I treated my Bible like one of those balls you shake, ask a question, flip over, and find your answer. Too many times I came to Scripture looking for an answer to my question, or I treated it like a yearbook—looking for all the pictures of myself.

Then, I began asking a different question, and my entire Bible study and life changed. I asked, "What does this say about God?" This shifted my perspective from a self-centered approach toward Scripture (where I am always asking, "What does this mean *to* me or *for* me?") to a God-centered approach—intentionally looking for and seeking out what each passage teaches me about God.

The Bible is not about me. It is first and foremost a book about God, and His name and character are written across every page. Our purpose on earth is to know God and make Him known, to love God and love others. But we can't love what we don't know; we can't worship what we don't know. And the primary way we know God is through His Word. The pursuit of knowledge about God is not optional; it's essential.

On the following pages, you will find two lists to help you: Names of God and Characteristics of God. It's not comprehensive, and there are spaces for you to add others as you discover more with each passage you read. Here are ways you can have a God-centered approach to your study:

- Ask, "What characteristics of God do I see in this passage?"

- Ask, "What names of God do I see in this passage?" (His names speak to His character.)

- Complete this sentence: Because God is _____, I can _____.

While there are different roles within the Trinity (God the Father, God the Son, and God the Holy Spirit), for the sake of simplicity, I study them as One. If you need further help, visit www.FeastingOnTruth.com for more information and resources.

names of God

Abba Father

Adonai *(Lord, Master)*

Alpha and Omega

Bread of Life

Chief Cornerstone

Creator

Deliverer

El Elyon *(The Most High God)*

El Olam *(The Everlasting God)*

El Roi *(The God Who Sees Me)*

El Shaddai *(The Lord God Almighty)*

Elohim

Everlasting Father

Great High Priest

Holy One

I AM

Immanuel

King of Kings

Lamb of God

Light of the World

Lion of Judah

Lord of Lords

Mighty God

Morning Star

Prince of Peace

Resurrection and the Life

Savior

Wonderful Counselor

Yahweh Amen *(The Lord is Truth)*

Yahweh Jireh *(The Lord Provides)*

Yahweh Nissi *(The Lord is my Banner)*

Yahweh-Raah *(The Lord is my Shepherd)*

Yahweh Rapha *(The Lord Heals)*

Yahweh Shalom *(The Lord is Peace)*

characteristics of God

Abounding in Steadfast Love

Compassionate

Deliberate

Faithful

Forgiving

Full of Grace

Good

Glorious

Gracious

Guide

Holy

Immutable *(Unchanging)*

Infinite

Invisible

Jealous

Just

Kind

Long-Suffering/Patient

Love

Merciful

Mighty

Omnipotent *(All-Powerful)*

Omnipresent

Omniscient *(All-Knowing)*

One

Perfect

Protector

Provider

Refuge/Help

Righteous

Self-Sufficient

Slow to Anger

Sovereign

Trustworthy

Truth

Wise

With Us

KNOWING GOD NOTES

SO YOU MAY

Believe

MAPS

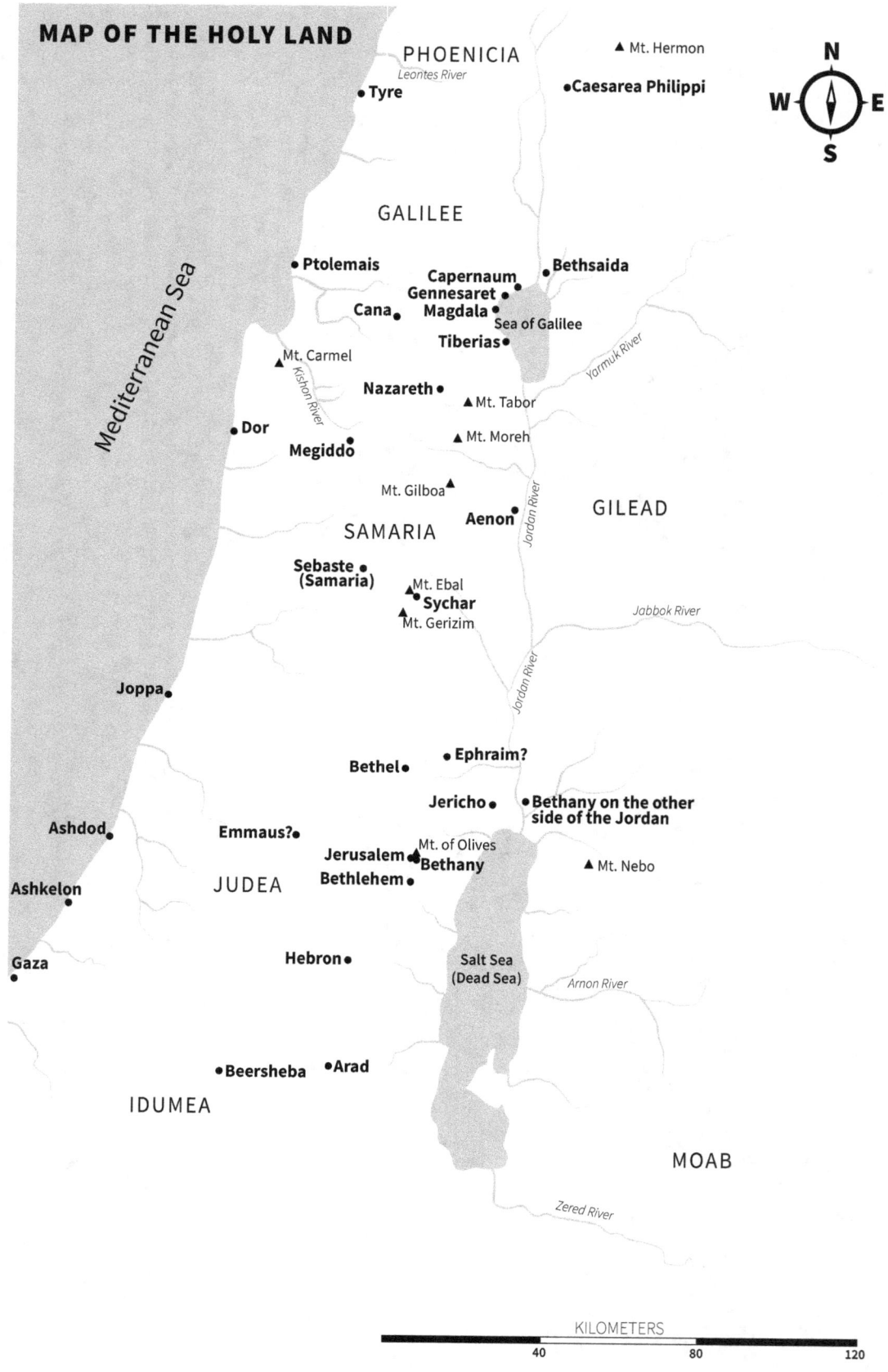

MAP OF THE HOLY LAND

PHOENICIA

Leontes River

▲ Mt. Hermon

• Tyre

• Caesarea Philippi

N
W E
S

GALILEE

• Ptolemais

Capernaum •
• Bethsaida

Gennesaret
Cana • Magdala •
Sea of Galilee
Tiberias •

Mt. Carmel ▲
Kishon River

Nazareth •
▲ Mt. Tabor

▲ Mt. Moreh
Yarmuk River

• Dor

Megiddo •
Mt. Gilboa ▲

Mediterranean Sea

SAMARIA
Aenon •
GILEAD

Jordan River

Sebaste • (Samaria)
Mt. Ebal ▲
Sychar
Mt. Gerizim ▲

Jabbok River

Joppa •

Jordan River

Bethel •
• Ephraim?

Jericho •
• Bethany on the other side of the Jordan

Ashdod •
Emmaus? •

Jerusalem • Mt. of Olives
Bethany
Bethlehem •

▲ Mt. Nebo

JUDEA

Ashkelon •

Hebron •
Salt Sea (Dead Sea)
Arnon River

Gaza •

• Beersheba • Arad

IDUMEA

MOAB

Zered River

KILOMETERS
40   80   120

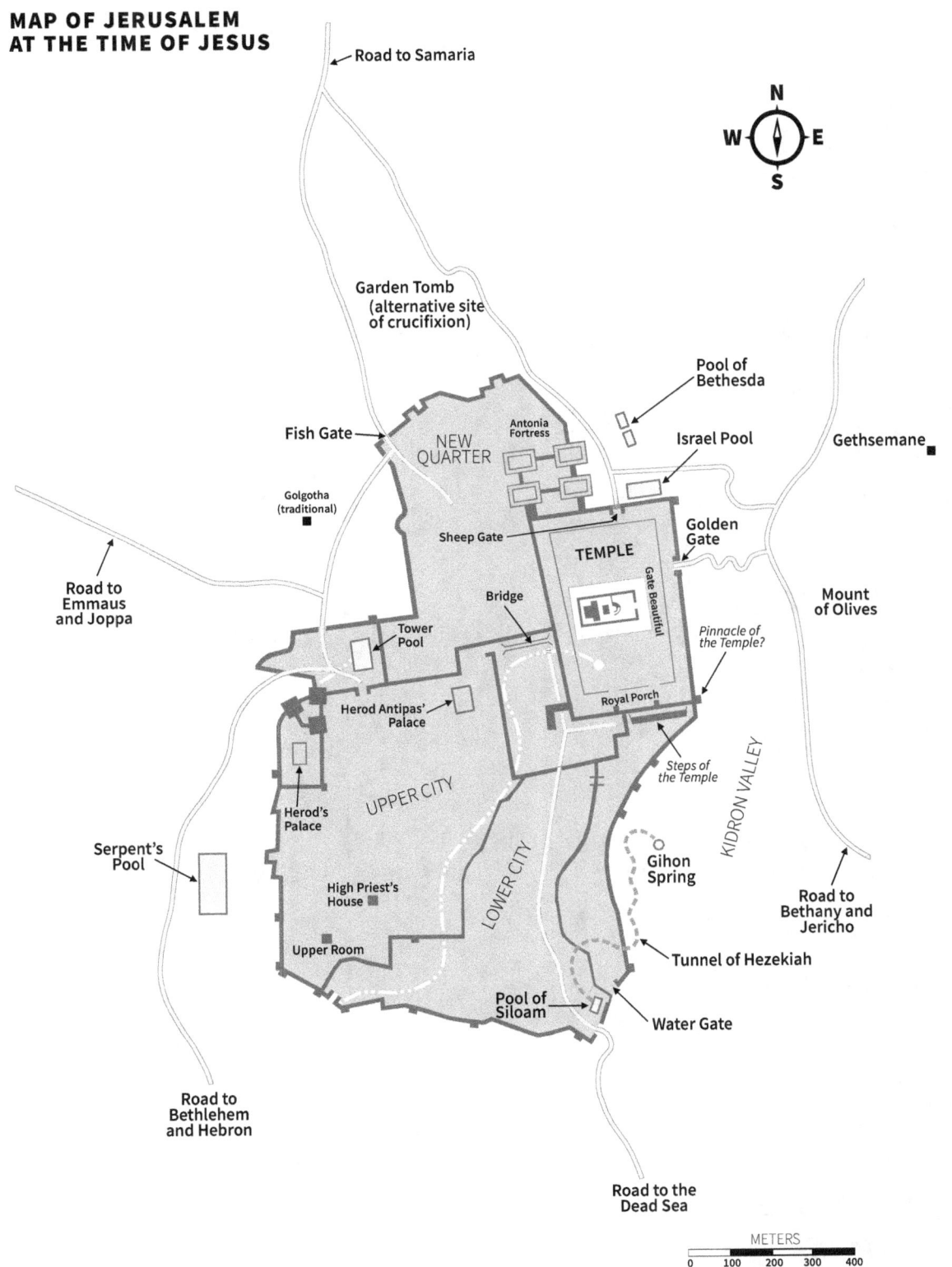

MAP OF JERUSALEM
AT THE TIME OF JESUS

Road to Samaria

N
W · E
S

Garden Tomb
(alternative site
of crucifixion)

Pool of
Bethesda

Fish Gate

NEW
QUARTER

Antonia
Fortress

Israel Pool

Gethsemane

Golgotha
(traditional)

Sheep Gate

TEMPLE

Golden
Gate

Road to
Emmaus
and Joppa

Bridge

Gate Beautiful

Mount
of Olives

Tower
Pool

Pinnacle of
the Temple?

Herod Antipas'
Palace

Royal Porch

Steps of
the Temple

KIDRON VALLEY

UPPER CITY

Herod's
Palace

Serpent's
Pool

LOWER CITY

Gihon
Spring

Road to
Bethany
and Jericho

High Priest's
House

Tunnel of Hezekiah

Upper Room

Pool of
Siloam

Water Gate

Road to
Bethlehem
and Hebron

Road to the
Dead Sea

METERS
0   100   200   300   400

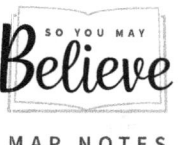

MAP NOTES

So You May

Believe

CONTEXT

Who wrote the Gospel of John?

What do you know about this author?

To whom was this book written?

When was it written?

What is the genre of this book?

What was the intent or purpose?

What was going on in history when it was written?

CONTEXT NOTES

CONTEXT NOTES

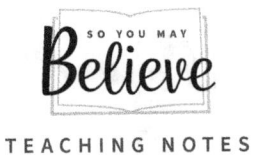

SO YOU MAY

Believe

TEACHING NOTES

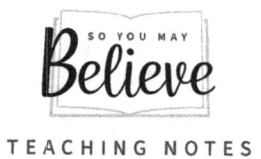

TEACHING NOTES

GROUP NOTES

GROUP NOTES

SO YOU MAY

Believe

JOHN 1

READ JOHN 1

WHAT DOES THIS SAY?

Write a 2–3 sentence summary of this passage.

Who? What? Where? When?

List any repeated words or phrases.

List any transitional words.

WHAT DOES THIS SAY ABOUT GOD?

What characteristics of God do you see in this passage?

WHAT DOES THIS MEAN?

Look up the following words in the dictionary and write out their definitions:

Glory:

Dwell:

_____:

_____:

CROSS-REFERENCES

Isaiah 40:3–5:

Colossians 1:15–20:

_____:

_____:

_____:

STARTER QUESTIONS

Compare John 1:1–14 with Genesis 1–2. How do these two passages parallel each other?

DISCUSSION: In vv. 1–14, what characteristics does John attribute to Jesus that were previously attributed only to God the Father?

What event did John the Baptist witness and testify to? According to John the Baptist, who is Jesus?

_____

_____

_____

Who are the four disciples Jesus calls in this passage?

_____

DISCUSSION: In what ways does John prove that Jesus is the fulfillment of the Old Testament in this chapter?

_____

_____

_____

_____

DISCUSSION: List the seven names or titles of Jesus given in vv. 35–51 and describe how each highlights different aspects of Jesus' call and ministry on earth.

_____

_____

_____

_____

_____

_____

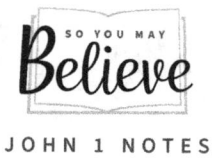

SO YOU MAY
Believe

JOHN 1 NOTES

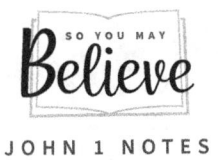

SO YOU MAY

Believe

JOHN 1 NOTES

HOW SHOULD I RESPOND?

How does this chapter grow your belief in Jesus and help you find life in His name?

Write a prayer of thanksgiving for who He is.

Because God is:

    I can:

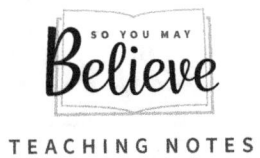

TEACHING NOTES

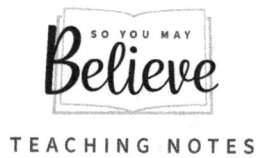

TEACHING NOTES

GROUP NOTES

GROUP NOTES

SO YOU MAY

Believe

JOHN 2

READ JOHN 2

WHAT DOES THIS SAY?

Write a 2–3 sentence summary of this passage.

Who? What? Where? When?

List any repeated words or phrases.

List any transitional words.

WHAT DOES THIS SAY ABOUT GOD?

What characteristics of God do you see in this passage?

WHAT DOES THIS MEAN?

Look up the following words in the dictionary and write out their definitions:

Sign:

Believe:

_____:

_____:

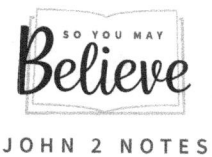
CROSS-REFERENCES

Isaiah 25:6–9:

Psalm 69:

————————————:

————————————:

————————————:

STARTER QUESTIONS

At the wedding at Cana, how many stone water jars were there? What were these used for?

What does Jesus tell the servants to do? How do they respond? What is the result?

DISCUSSION: How have you seen complete obedience lead to glory for God in your life?

JOHN 2 NOTES

Which festival was approaching when Jesus went to Jerusalem? What event in Jewish history did this festival commemorate (see Deuteronomy 16:1–8)?

What did Jesus say the merchants had turned the temple into? What did this mean?

DISCUSSION: The disciples recalled Psalm 69:9. How would this psalm resonate with the original audience?

DISCUSSION: When Jesus predicted the destruction of the temple, what temple was He talking about? Again recalling John's intent and the original audience, what does he convey about Jesus?

DISCUSSION: Twice John noted that the disciples "remembered" (vv. 17, 22), and it strengthened their faith. What helps us remember God's Word in a way that strengthens our faith?

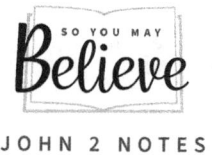

JOHN 2 NOTES

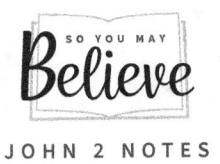

SO YOU MAY

Believe

JOHN 2 NOTES

HOW SHOULD I RESPOND?

How does this chapter grow your belief in Jesus and help you find life in His name?

Write a prayer of thanksgiving for who He is.

Because God is:

     I can:

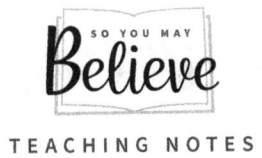

SO YOU MAY

Believe

TEACHING NOTES

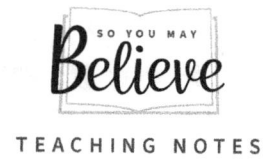

SO YOU MAY

Believe

TEACHING NOTES

GROUP NOTES

GROUP NOTES

SO YOU MAY

Believe

JOHN 3

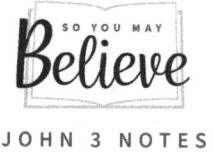
READ JOHN 3

WHAT DOES THIS SAY?

Write a 2–3 sentence summary of this passage.

Who? What? Where? When?

List any repeated words or phrases.

List any transitional words.

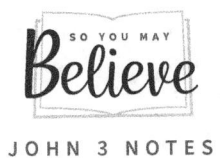
WHAT DOES THIS SAY ABOUT GOD?

What characteristics of God do you see in this passage?

WHAT DOES THIS MEAN?

Look up the following words in the dictionary and write out their definitions:

Witness:

Truth:

_____:

_____:

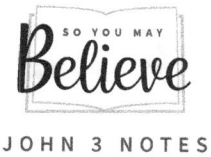
CROSS-REFERENCES

2 Corinthians 5:16–21:

Hebrews 11:1–3:

_____ :

_____ :

_____ :

STARTER QUESTIONS

Who comes to meet with Jesus? When did he come?

Who were the Pharisees?

DISCUSSION: Read Numbers 21:4–9. How does the story of the Bronze Serpent parallel Jesus?

Write out John 3:16–17. Why did Jesus come here?

DISCUSSION: How do these Old Testament passages add understanding to this chapter?

Ezekiel 36:22–32:

Proverbs 30:1–6:

How does John the Baptist respond to his disciples leaving to follow Jesus? To what does he compare himself?

DISCUSSION: How are truth and light related?

DISCUSSION: How do we escape the wrath of God and receive salvation?

SO YOU MAY

Believe

JOHN 3 NOTES

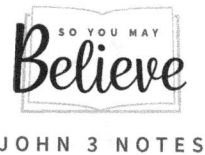

HOW SHOULD I RESPOND?

How does this chapter grow your belief in Jesus and help you find life in His name?

Write a prayer of thanksgiving for who He is.

Because God is:

    I can:

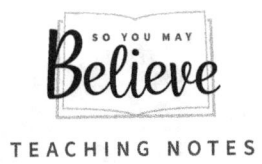

SO YOU MAY

Believe

TEACHING NOTES

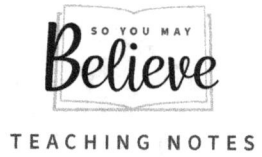

TEACHING NOTES

GROUP NOTES

GROUP NOTES

SO YOU MAY

Believe

JOHN 4

READ JOHN 4

WHAT DOES THIS SAY?

Write a 2–3 sentence summary of this passage.

Who? What? Where? When?

List any repeated words or phrases.

List any transitional words.

WHAT DOES THIS SAY ABOUT GOD?

What characteristics of God do you see in this passage?

WHAT DOES THIS MEAN?

Look up the following words in the dictionary and write out their definitions:

Worship:

Thirsty:

_____:

_____:

CROSS-REFERENCES

Romans 12:1–2:

_____:

_____:

_____:

STARTER QUESTIONS

What historical site is in Sychar?

What does Jesus say to the woman in vv. 13–14?

How do these Old and New Testament passages add understanding to this chapter:

Isaiah 44:1–5:

Jeremiah 2:11–13:

Zechariah 14:8–9:

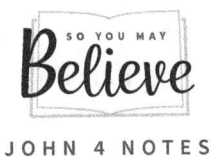
Revelation 21:1–7:

Revelation 22:1–5:

Find Sychar on the map on page 22. What are the names of the two mountains on either side of this town?

DISCUSSION: Read Deuteronomy 11:26–32, Deuteronomy 27–28, and Joshua 8:30–35. Why are these mountains significant? What does each represent?

DISCUSSION: What does Jesus reveal to this woman in vv. 25–26? Why is this significant?

What is the result of the woman's testimony?

Write out Revelation 12:11. Why is it important that we share what God has done for us? How does the story of the official's son further prove this?

DISCUSSION: How does knowing Jesus and His Word are true and trustworthy affect the way we live our lives every day?

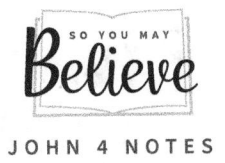

SO YOU MAY
Believe

JOHN 4 NOTES

<u>HOW SHOULD I RESPOND?</u>

How does this chapter grow your belief in Jesus and help you find life in His name?

Write a prayer of thanksgiving for who He is.

Because God is:

    I can:

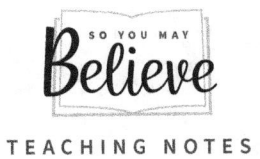

TEACHING NOTES

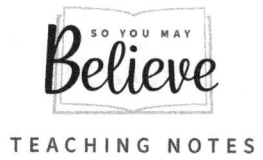

TEACHING NOTES

GROUP NOTES

GROUP NOTES

SO YOU MAY
Believe

JOHN 5

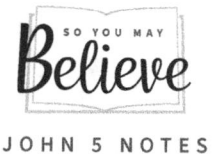

READ JOHN 5

WHAT DOES THIS SAY?

Write a 2–3 sentence summary of this passage.

Who? What? Where? When?

List any repeated words or phrases.

List any transitional words.

WHAT DOES THIS SAY ABOUT GOD?

What characteristics of God do you see in this passage?

WHAT DOES THIS MEAN?

Look up the following words in the dictionary and write out their definitions:

Sabbath:

Life:

_____:

_____:

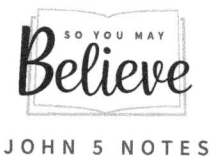

CROSS-REFERENCES

Daniel 7:13–14:

_____

_____

Exodus 20:8–11:

_____

_____

_____:

_____

_____:

_____

STARTER QUESTIONS

On what day did the Jesus heal the sick man?

DISCUSSION: Read Exodus 16. This is the first place Sabbath is mentioned in Scripture. Based on this story, what is the purpose of Sabbath?

What does Jesus say to the man later in the temple?

How did the sick man respond to Jesus healing him?

DISCUSSION: In context of vv. 19–29, what awaits those who do not believe? What hope is there for those who believe in Jesus?

DISCUSSION: How do these New Testament verses add understanding to this chapter?

1 Peter 3:18:

Ephesians 2:1–7:

Colossians 2:13–23:

DISCUSSION: In what ways does Jesus say He and the Father are One?

DISCUSSION: In vv. 31–47, what five witnesses does Jesus give to confirm His identity?

DISCUSSION: Read Luke 24:13–35 and write out v. 27. Together with John 5, what is the Old Testament about? What did Jesus come to do?

JOHN 5 NOTES

JOHN 5 NOTES

HOW SHOULD I RESPOND?

How does this chapter grow your belief in Jesus and help you find life in His name?

Write a prayer of thanksgiving for who He is.

Because God is:

    I can:

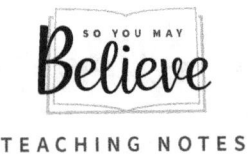

TEACHING NOTES

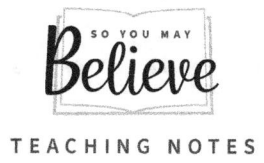

SO YOU MAY

Believe

TEACHING NOTES

GROUP NOTES

GROUP NOTES

SO YOU MAY
Believe

JOHN 6

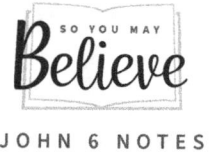
READ JOHN 6

WHAT DOES THIS SAY?

Write a 2–3 sentence summary of this passage.

Who? What? Where? When?

List any repeated words or phrases.

List any transitional words.

SO YOU MAY

Believe

JOHN 6 NOTES

WHAT DOES THIS SAY ABOUT GOD?

What characteristics of God do you see in this passage?

WHAT DOES THIS MEAN?

Look up the following words in the dictionary and write out their definitions:

Thanks:

Fill:

_____:

_____:

CROSS-REFERENCES

Isaiah 55:1-5:

Jeremiah 31:33–34:

_____:

_____:

STARTER QUESTIONS

What feast is at hand? What do you know about this feast? (see your notes on John 2)

How much did the people eat in vv. 1–15? How many baskets were leftover?

DISCUSSION: What does the story of Jesus walking on water reveal about Jesus' identity?

Why were the people seeking Jesus in vv. 22–27?

What is the purpose of food?

Read Exodus 3:13–15. What is God's name?

The first "I AM" statement in John:

DISCUSSION: When Jesus uses God's name, what is He saying about Himself?

DISCUSSION: Read Exodus 16. How is Jesus like manna? How is the "bread" He provides better?

DISCUSSION: What are the earthly things we depend on to give us what only Jesus can?

How do some of the people/disciples respond to Jesus? How do the twelve disciples respond?

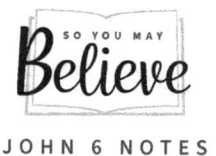

JOHN 6 NOTES

JOHN 6 NOTES

HOW SHOULD I RESPOND?

How does this chapter grow your belief in Jesus and help you find life in His name?

Write a prayer of thanksgiving for who He is.

Because God is:

      I can:

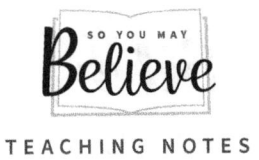

TEACHING NOTES

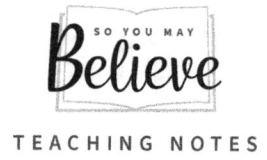

TEACHING NOTES

SO YOU MAY

Believe

GROUP NOTES

GROUP NOTES

SO YOU MAY

Believe

JOHN 7

READ JOHN 7

<u>WHAT DOES THIS SAY?</u>

Write a 2–3 sentence summary of this passage.

Who? What? Where? When?

List any repeated words or phrases.

List any transitional words.

WHAT DOES THIS SAY ABOUT GOD?

What characteristics of God do you see in this passage?

WHAT DOES THIS MEAN?

Look up the following words in the dictionary and write out their definitions:

Authority:

Know:

_____:

_____:

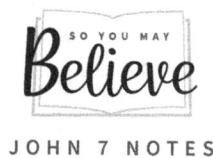

CROSS-REFERENCES

Zechariah 14:6–9:

Micah 5:2–5a:

_____:

_____:

STARTER QUESTIONS

What feast is at hand?

DISCUSSION: What details do you learn about this feast from these Old Testament passages?

Leviticus 23:33–43:

Deuteronomy 16:13–15:

Deuteronomy 31:9–13:

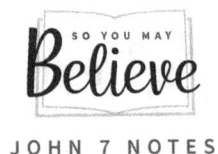
Ezra 3:1–6:

Nehemiah 8:13–18:

Who do the people and the religious leaders say Jesus is? (hint: there are many!)

Who speaks up in defense of Jesus in v. 50?

DISCUSSION: What does Jesus say on the last day of the feast?

What does the living water represent?
DISCUSSION: How do these Old Testament cross-references add to your understanding of living water and what Jesus offers us?

Isaiah 12:1–6:

SO YOU MAY

Believe

JOHN 7 NOTES

Isaiah 55:

Ezekiel 47:1–12:

DISCUSSION: Read Revelation 22:1–5, 17. What future hope does living water represent?

SO YOU MAY

Believe

JOHN 7 NOTES

HOW SHOULD I RESPOND?

How does this chapter grow your belief in Jesus and help you find life in His name?

Write a prayer of thanksgiving for who He is.

Because God is:

     I can:

TEACHING NOTES

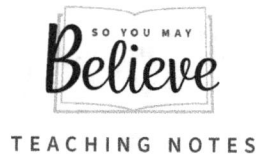

SO YOU MAY

Believe

TEACHING NOTES

GROUP NOTES

GROUP NOTES

SO YOU MAY
Believe

JOHN 8

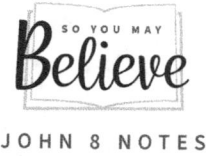

READ JOHN 8

WHAT DOES THIS SAY?

Write a 2–3 sentence summary of this passage.

Who? What? Where? When?

List any repeated words or phrases.

List any transitional words.

WHAT DOES THIS SAY ABOUT GOD?

What characteristics of God do you see in this passage?

WHAT DOES THIS MEAN?

Look up the following words in the dictionary and write out their definitions:

Abide:

Disciples:

Liar:

_____:

CROSS-REFERENCES

Deuteronomy 17:6:

Isaiah 40:8:

_____ :

_____ :

STARTER QUESTIONS

The second "I AM" statement in John:

Revisit the connection of light and truth from John 1:5 and John 3:16–21. How does John 8 build upon this?

DISCUSSION: Contrast the character of Jesus and the character of the devil.

The Character of Jesus	The Character of the Devil

DISCUSSION: What actions mark Jesus' disciples?

DISCUSSION: What actions mark those who will not believe?

DISCUSSION: How do these prophecies from Isaiah add to your understanding of this passage?

Isaiah 42:1–9:

Isaiah 43:8–13:

Isaiah 52:13–53:6:

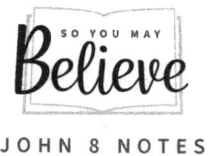

JOHN 8 NOTES

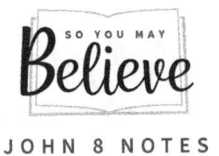

SO YOU MAY

Believe

JOHN 8 NOTES

HOW SHOULD I RESPOND?

How does this chapter grow your belief in Jesus and help you find life in His name?

Write a prayer of thanksgiving for who He is.

Because God is:

      I can:

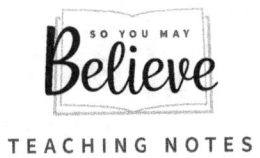

TEACHING NOTES

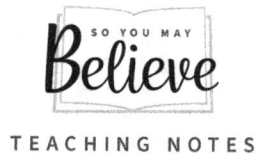

TEACHING NOTES

GROUP NOTES

GROUP NOTES

SO YOU MAY

Believe

JOHN 9

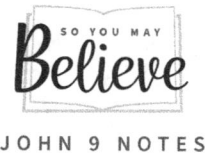
READ JOHN 9

WHAT DOES THIS SAY?

Write a 2–3 sentence summary of this passage.

Who? What? Where? When?

List any repeated words or phrases.

List any transitional words.

WHAT DOES THIS SAY ABOUT GOD?

What characteristics of God do you see in this passage?

WHAT DOES THIS MEAN?

Look up the following words in the dictionary and write out their definitions:

Sin:

Blind:

_____:

_____:

CROSS-REFERENCES

Psalm 34:15–16:

Psalm 145:19–20:

_____:

_____:

_____:

STARTER QUESTIONS

What question do the disciples ask concerning the man born blind?

How does Jesus respond?

DISCUSSION: How have you seen God use suffering for your good and His glory in your life?

Where does Jesus tell the blind man to go wash?

DISCUSSION: How do these Old Testament passages add to your understanding of this passage?

    Ezekiel 18:20–23:

    Isaiah 35:

    Revisit the Isaiah prophecies from John 8:

Why do the blind man's parents not speak up to the religious leaders? What happens to the man born blind after he speaks to the religious leaders? How might this passage and Jesus' words in vv. 35–41 encourage the original audience?

DISCUSSION: Read Romans 9:30–10:4 and Isaiah 28:14–16. Who is truly blind in John 9? Who are those that see?

JOHN 9 NOTES

SO YOU MAY

Believe

JOHN 9 NOTES

HOW SHOULD I RESPOND?

How does this chapter grow your belief in Jesus and help you find life in His name?

Write a prayer of thanksgiving for who He is.

Because God is:

    I can:

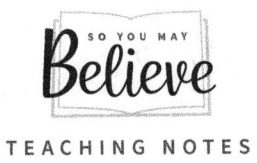

TEACHING NOTES

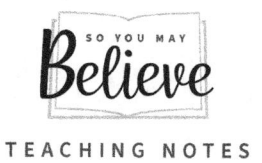

TEACHING NOTES

GROUP NOTES

GROUP NOTES

SO YOU MAY
Believe

JOHN 10

READ JOHN 10

WHAT DOES THIS SAY?

Write a 2–3 sentence summary of this passage.

Who? What? Where? When?

List any repeated words or phrases.

List any transitional words.

WHAT DOES THIS SAY ABOUT GOD?

What characteristics of God do you see in this passage?

WHAT DOES THIS MEAN?

Look up the following words in the dictionary and write out their definitions:

Good:

Blasphemy:

_____:

_____:

CROSS-REFERENCES

Hebrews 3:7–14:

1 Peter 2:1–10:

_____ :

_____ :

_____ :

STARTER QUESTIONS

The third "I AM" statement in John:

The fourth "I AM" statement in John:

Who is the Good Shepherd? What does the Good Shepherd do?

Who are the sheep? What do the sheep do?

Who is the thief? What does the thief do?

What is the abundant life Jesus promises in v. 10?

DISCUSSION: What do these psalms teach about God as our Good Shepherd and Door/Gate and our response to Him?

Psalm 118: _____

_____

Psalm 23: _____

_____

Psalm 100: _____

_____

Psalm 95: _____

_____

DISCUSSION: Read Ezekiel 34. How does John 10 show Jesus as the fulfillment of that prophecy?

_____

_____

_____

_____

_____

_____

_____

_____

SO YOU MAY

Believe

JOHN 10 NOTES

HOW SHOULD I RESPOND?

How does this chapter grow your belief in Jesus and help you find life in His name?

Write a prayer of thanksgiving for who He is.

Because God is:

    I can:

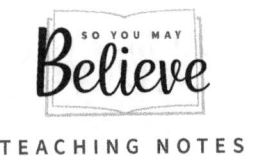

TEACHING NOTES

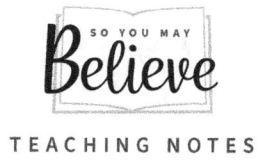

TEACHING NOTES

GROUP NOTES

GROUP NOTES

ADDITIONAL NOTES

ADDITIONAL NOTES

ADDITIONAL NOTES

ADDITIONAL NOTES

feasting at the table

I love hearty food. I've never been the girl to order a salad; give me the burger. But hearty doesn't necessarily mean unhealthy. This chili uses lean ground meat and loads up on the vegetables. It's one of my go-to favorites and perfect when you need to feed a crowd (or want a meal with leftovers).

You can use ground turkey, lean ground beef, or ground chicken for this recipe. Even using lean meats, this chili packs a lot of flavor! The carrots add a sweet balance to the smoky heat of the chili powder. The bell peppers add heartiness and a touch of crunch. But the real secret is the chocolate at the end. I know, I know. It sounds weird, but adding the unsweetened chocolate to finish it off brings a dark warmth that you can't get from any other ingredient. And what I love about this recipe is that it is super flexible. Want more bell peppers? You can add more. Don't like black beans? Switch them out for kidney or pinto or delete the beans altogether. If you like spicy chili, you can add a dash of hot sauce or use a hot chili powder instead of mild. This is your canvas, and you can create the dish that best meets your needs.

The customization doesn't stop there; then there are the toppings! Shredded cheddar cheese, sour cream, avocado, corn chips, hot sauce, or raw onion all make great toppings. You can also make some cornbread to serve on the side. The possibilities are endless! A quick note about cheese: it's worth it to buy a block and shred it yourself. Commercially grated cheese is typically coated in anti-caking agents, so it won't melt as well. It's also typically less expensive ounce for ounce to buy a block of cheese vs. shredded in bags.

I hope you enjoy this flexible and delicious dish. Happy feasting!

ERIN'S CHILI

Time: About an hour
Yield: 6–8 servings

INGREDIENTS
2 tablespoons extra virgin olive oil
3 large carrots, chopped
1 large yellow or sweet onion, chopped
2 pounds lean ground beef, turkey, or chicken
4 cloves of garlic, finely chopped
3 bell peppers, chopped (red, orange, or yellow)
1 tablespoon Cumin
3 tablespoons mild chili powder
1 tablespoon tomato paste
1-28 ounce can crushed tomatoes (preferably no salt added)
1-15 ounce can tomato sauce (preferably no salt added)
1-15 ounce can of beans (black, kidney, or pinto), drained and rinsed.
1 ounce unsweetened chocolate
Kosher salt

INSTRUCTIONS
1. Heat 2 tablespoons of extra virgin olive oil in a Dutch oven or large, heavy bottom pot over medium heat.
2. Add carrots and onions. Cook until carrots begin to soften and onions begin to brown (about 10 minutes), stirring occasionally.
3. Add ground meat and cook until no longer pink, stirring occasionally.
4. Add 1 teaspoon of kosher salt and the garlic. Stir and cook one more minute.
5. Add the chopped bell peppers. Stir and cook another 2–3 minutes.
6. Add cumin, chili powder, and tomato paste. Stir and cook for one minute to bloom the spices.
7. Stir in the crushed tomatoes, tomato sauce, and beans.
8. Add another teaspoon of kosher salt. Cover and simmer for at least 20 minutes, stirring occasionally. The longer it simmers, the more flavorful it will be.
9. Add more kosher salt to taste.
10. Just before serving, add the chocolate, stirring until melted and incorporated.
11. Serve and top with your favorite toppings: cilantro, corn chips, sour cream, avocado, shredded cheese. And don't forget the cornbread!

about Erin

ERIN H. WARREN is an author, Bible teacher, and speaker. Her ministry, Feasting on Truth, provides in-depth Bible studies for individuals, small groups, and churches. With an intentional focus on exploring the character of God, she encourages and guides others as they build confidence in studying the Bible. She is the author of *Feasting on Truth: Savor the Life-giving Word of God* and *Everyday Prayers for Faith: Finding Confidence in God No Matter What*, and many Bible studies. She and her husband, Kris, have three littles (who aren't so little anymore), and they live in Central Florida. She loves a house full of people and a table full of food and hopes tacos never go out of style. You can find more information about Feasting on Truth on her website: FeastingOnTruth.com. You can also connect with her on Instagram: @erinhwarren and @feastingontruth and YouTube: www.youtube.com/c/erinhwarren.

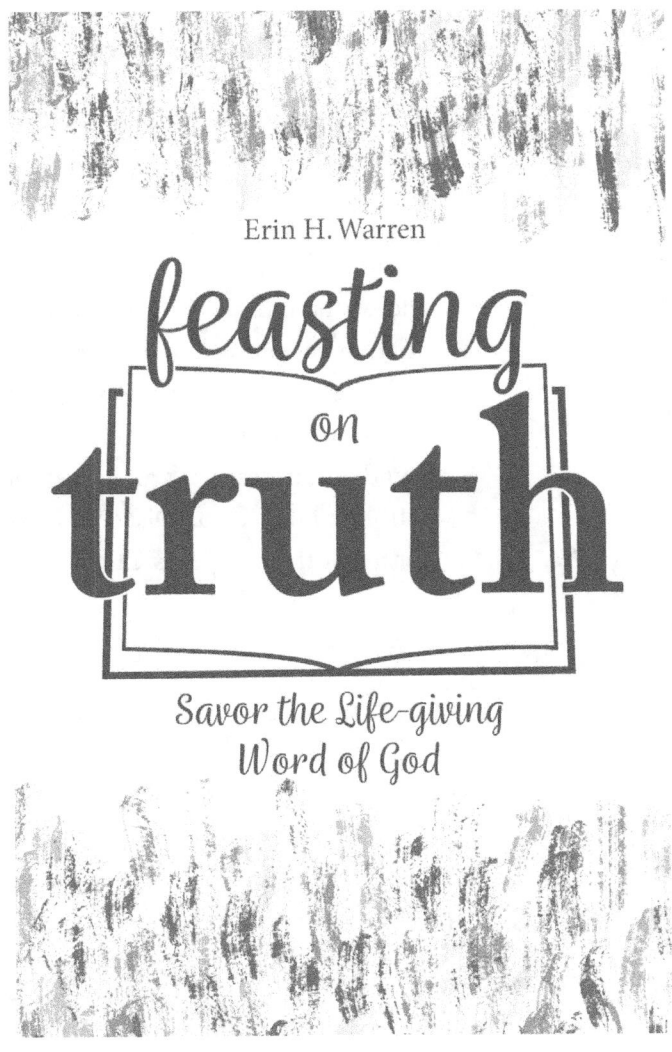

Erin H. Warren

FEASTING ON TRUTH

SAVOR THE LIFE-GIVING WORD OF GOD

We know reading the Bible is important, but sometimes it's hard to know where to start or how to make sense of these ancient words. For years, Erin Warren struggled to do the same. Then she found a simple approach that changed everything.

As she shares her own story, Erin guides the reader to a deeper understanding of why we need to study Scripture and how to do it. Her desire is to encourage and equip women to discover God's truths for themselves.

The word *feast* is rooted in abundance. That is what awaits us in the pages of Scripture: a table laid out before us, not only for our essential nourishment, but for our enjoyment.

FeastingOnTruth.com/Books

TO DWELL IN OUR MIDST

A STUDY OF THE TABERNACLE AND HOW IT POINTS US TO JESUS

Why study this ancient tent? What does knowing about the Tabernacle have to do with our faith on this side of the cross? Everything. This tent is not merely ritual or history or good information—it's essential to understanding our salvation. Our detailed and deliberate God gave us the Tabernacle because one day, He would give us Jesus. It's an invitation into a relationship with our Holy God. Discover God's plan to dwell in our midst through Jesus Christ.

FeastingOnTruth.com/Dwell

STORIES FROM THE WILDERNESS

A STUDY OF THE ISRAELITES' JOURNEY FROM EGYPT TO THE PROMISED LAND

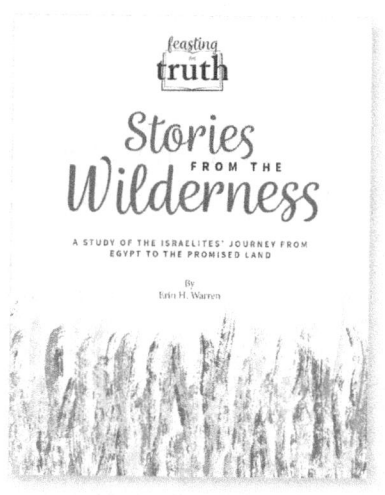

The wilderness. It is a place that feels hard, empty, lifeless, and pathless, and it often leaves us with questions about who God is. But where we see a place that is worthless, confusing, and chaotic, God sees a place to display His power. Time and time again throughout Scripture, God takes the worthless, seemingly wasteful, confusing, chaotic, and empty places and uses them as a backdrop to prove His character, draw us in, and display His glory.

FeastingOnTruth.com/Wilderness

WAY MAKER

AN ADVENT STUDY THROUGH THE BOOK OF HEBREWS

Jesus' coming was more than giving us forgiveness of sins or to part the way before us. He came to part the divide between God and us, between us and heaven. Jesus is the One who made a way to a restored relationship with God. No other book gives us a more comprehensive view of Jesus as our Way Maker than the book of Hebrews.

FeastingOnTruth.com/WayMaker

LIGHT & LIFE

AN INDUCTIVE BIBLE STUDY ON PSALM 119

We hear it all the time: we need to read the Bible every day. But why is it so important that we know, understand, and apply this ancient book to our lives today? What's in it for us? In Psalm 119, we see over and over that God's Word brings life, and it's a light to guide us. If we truly knew the power the Word of God has in our lives, we wouldn't be able to put it down.

FeastingOnTruth.com/LightAndLife

BY HIS GRACE FOR HIS GLORY
AN INDUCTIVE BIBLE STUDY ON THE BOOK OF ROMANS

Romans is foundational yet deep. It's hard to understand yet simple. It is an incredibly powerful book that has been changing lives for centuries, and the truths in these sixteen chapters have the power to change our faith too. There are many familiar verses in Romans, and we associate this book with evangelism. But it is so much more! Discover what it looks like to live by His grace for His glory.

FeastingOnTruth.com/Romans

UNEXPECTED SAVIOR
AN INDUCTIVE BIBLE STUDY ON THE GOSPEL OF MARK

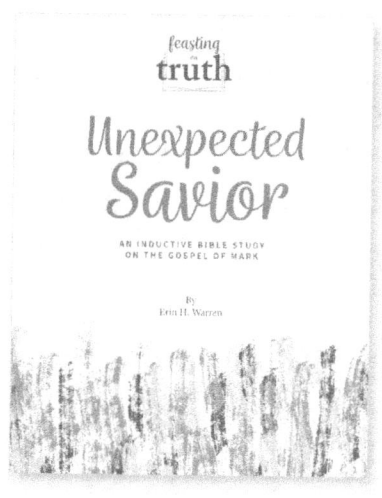

The Gospel of Mark challenges the expected ideal of the Messiah—not a conquering king or a wish-granting genie, but rather a man of sorrows and a suffering servant. This short yet impactful account of Jesus' life reveals the character of the One who came to save us. Jesus mourned the brokenness around Him: the sickness, the pain, the hardness of heart. He grew angry at the sin of those who led His sheep astray. He was the One who came not to be served, but to serve. He came to prove the faithfulness of God and provide unshakable hope as we walk through hardships.

FeastingOnTruth.com/Mark

STEADFAST

AN INDUCTIVE BIBLE STUDY ON 1 & 2 PETER

Peter knew suffering, but Peter also knew Jesus. If there was anyone who could understand suffering and the call to steadfast faith, it was Peter. These letters are an encouragement to anyone facing hardships and trials, a reminder of what is true, and a guide to stand firm in faith no matter what. Peter reminds us that we can be steadfast because our God is steadfast. And when we are, what awaits us in eternity is worth far more than anything this world has to offer.

FeastingOnTruth.com/Peter

www.ingramcontent.com/pod-product-compliance
Lightning Source LLC
Chambersburg PA
CBHW081329120626
46546CB00011B/3273